**Cranbury Public Library**
23 North Main St., Cranbury, NJ 08512
(609) 655-0555    f: (609) 655-2858

www.CranburyPublicLibrary.org

# UNITED STATES TENNIS ASSOCIATION

BY DAVID RAUSCH

EPIC

BELLWETHER MEDIA • MINNEAPOLIS, MN

**EPIC BOOKS** are no ordinary books. They burst with intense action, high-speed heroics, and shadows of the unknown. Are you ready for an Epic adventure?

This edition first published in 2015 by Bellwether Media, Inc.

No part of this publication may be reproduced in whole or in part without written permission of the publisher. For information regarding permission, write to Bellwether Media, Inc., Attention: Permissions Department, 5357 Penn Avenue South, Minneapolis, MN 55419.

Library of Congress Cataloging-in-Publication Data

Rausch, David.
  United States Tennis Association / by David Rausch.
    pages cm. – (Epic. Major League Sports)
  Includes bibliographical references and index.
  Summary: "Engaging images accompany information about the United States Tennis Association. The combination of high-interest subject matter and light text is intended for students in grades 2 through 7"– Provided by publisher.
  ISBN 978-1-62617-138-1 (hardcover : alk. paper)
  1. United States Tennis Association–Juvenile literature. 2. Tennis–United States–History–Juvenile literature.  I. Title.
  GV996.5.R37 2014
  796.342–dc23
                                    2014014389

Printed in the United States of America, North Mankato, MN.

# TABLE OF CONTENTS

# WHAT IS THE USTA?

The United States Tennis Association (USTA) supports tennis in the U.S. It is the largest tennis **league** in the world!

# BECOME A MEMBER

Anyone can join the USTA. It has over 700,000 members.

Tennis players of all ages belong to the USTA. **Amateurs** go to camps and play in tournaments. The best players compete on the **Pro Circuit**.

# HISTORY OF THE USTA

The USTA was formed in 1881. It was called the United States National Lawn Tennis Association. The name changed in 1975.

# A LOOK BACK

**May 21, 1881:** The United States National Lawn Tennis Association is formed.

**August 31, 1881:** The first U.S. Open Championships are held in Newport, Rhode Island.

**1889:** Women players first play in the USTA.

**1892:** The first USTA mixed doubles championships are played.

**1920:** The league shortens its name to United States Lawn Tennis Association.

**1943:** The School Tennis Development Committee forms to promote tennis among young people in the U.S.

**September 13, 1954:** The International Tennis Hall of Fame opens in Newport, Rhode Island.

**1975:** The name is shortened again. It is now called the United States Tennis Association.

**November 8, 1978:** The USTA oversees the U.S. players in the Olympics.

**1979:** The USTA launches the Pro Circuit.

**1983:** The National Schools Program starts to bring tennis into schools.

**International Tennis Hall of Fame**

# PLAYING THE GAME

Every tennis **match** starts with a **serve**. Two players or pairs **rally** for the point. A **chair umpire** watches for the ball to land outside the court.

chair umpire

# TWICE THE FUN

**Matches can be played by singles or doubles.**

A player or pair must score four points to win a **game**. The first to win six games takes a **set**. The first to win two or three sets wins the match.

## SCORING POINTS

Tennis has an odd scoring system. Love is zero points. Then it goes to 15, 30, 40, and game.

# TENNIS TALK

**ace**—when a serve lands in-bounds and the other player is not able to return it; 1 point for the server

**ad in**—when the server wins the first point after deuce; ad is short for advantage.

**ad out**—when the receiver wins the first point after deuce; ad is short for advantage.

**deuce**—when the score is 40-40; a player must win 2 points in a row to win the game.

**double fault**—when a player has two faults in a row; 1 point for the opponent

**fault**—when a player serves the ball out of bounds; a player gets a second try after a fault.

**let**—when a point must be replayed

**love all**—when the score is 0-0; a match begins at love all.

**match point**—when scoring the next point can win the match

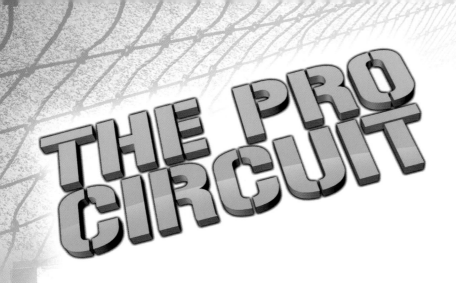

# THE PRO CIRCUIT

The USTA started the Pro Circuit in 1979. Here, skilled players compete for money and **rankings**. It is the path to the **Grand Slams**.

# INTERNATIONAL PLAY

**Players from more than 50 countries play in Pro Circuit events.**

Players get points for wins in the Pro Circuit. They are ranked based on these points. The best make it to the Grand Slams.

**BEST OF THE BEST**

Roger Federer was the top ranked tennis player for 237 weeks in a row. That is longer than any other player!

# THE U.S. OPEN

The USTA hosts the U.S. Open every year. It is the fourth Grand Slam. The others are the Australian Open, French Open, and Wimbledon.

# A GRAND COURT

The U.S. Open is held at the USTA Billie Jean King National Tennis Center. This is in New York City.

The U.S. Open lasts for two weeks in August and September. Players compete in singles, doubles, or **mixed doubles** events. The singles champions win the U.S. Open Cup!

# GLOSSARY

**amateurs**—athletes who play a sport for fun

**chair umpire**—a person who sits in a tall chair to watch the ball and enforce the rules

**game**—a division within a tennis set

**Grand Slams**—the four important tennis tournaments; the Grand Slams are also called the Majors.

**league**—a group of people or teams united by a common interest or activity

**match**—a tennis contest made up of sets

**mixed doubles**—matches between teams consisting of one man and one woman

**Pro Circuit**—professional tennis events

**rally**—to hit the ball back and forth across a net

**rankings**—positions that reflect skill and success

**serve**—the first shot that begins each point

**set**—a division within a tennis match

# TO LEARN MORE

## At the Library

Carr, Aaron. *Tennis*. New York, N.Y.: AV2 by Weigl, 2013.

Savage, Jeff. *Roger Federer*. Minneapolis, Minn.: Lerner Publications, 2009.

Wendorff, Anne. *Tennis*. Minneapolis, Minn.: Bellwether Media, 2010.

## On the Web

Learning more about the United States Tennis Association is as easy as 1, 2, 3.

1. Go to www.factsurfer.com.

2. Enter "United States Tennis Association" into the search box.

3. Click the "Surf" button and you will see a list of related web sites.

With factsurfer.com, finding more information is just a click away.

# INDEX

The images in this book are reproduced through the courtesy of: Neale Cousland, front cover (left, top right), pp. 6, 12, 16-17; Maxisport, pp. 4-5; microgen, p. 7; Hulton-Deutsch Collection/ Corbis, p. 8; Joy Brown, p. 9; John G. Mablango/ epa/ Corbis, p. 10; lev radin, pp. 11, 18, 19, 20, 21 (left, right); Rena Schild, p. 14; Tony Bowler, p. 15.